Interior Landscape
Copyright © Miguel Balaguer & Juan Balaguer, Estate of
Mirta Rosenberg, 2023
Translation Copyright © Yaki Setton & Sergio Waisman, 2023

Originally published in Spanish as *El paisaje interior*
(Buenos Aires: Bajo la luna, 2012)

ISBN 978-1-946604-17-0
First Edition, First Printing, 2023

Ugly Duckling Presse
The Old American Can Factory
232 Third Street #E-303
Brooklyn, NY 11215
www.uglyducklingpresse.org

INTERIOR LANDSCAPE
EL PAISAJE INTERIOR

Mirta Rosenberg

translated by Yaki Setton and Sergio Waisman

UGLY DUCKLING PRESSE

Contents

Things That Become Names
(Cosas que se vuelven nombres)
11

Interior Landscape
(El paisaje interior)
45

Intimate Bestiary
(Bestiario íntimo)
87

Conversos
111

**The Eye of the I:
Translating Mirta Rosenberg**
by Yaki Setton & Sergio Waisman
151

**Biographical Notes
& Acknowledgments**
161

THINGS THAT BECOME NAMES
COSAS QUE SE VUELVEN NOMBRES

*things have become names,
thus* cow, Job

*but listen: it was still a maladjusted being, in constant
wait of something very pleasant to happen*

*cosas se han vuelto nombres,
así* vaca, Job

*pero oye: siguió siendo un ser inadaptado, en espera
constante de que algo muy grato ocurriese*

Olvido García Valdés

Yo

Haciendo del error virtud,
estoy donde mi cabeza estuvo y vio todo
hasta donde alcanzaba la vista,
porque ella —no yo— nunca se perdió:

en la entrevista oscuridad
del túnel, adelante, dio a pensar
—haciendo de virtud verdad— que esa cabeza
era todo el acontecimiento de la luz.

Y ella acontecía mientras yo
dentro del cuerpo me encerraba,
haciendo de cada órgano mi casa:
oeste o este era un todo sin ventanas,

una feliz ciudad descentrada
en la cuadrícula de la ocasión.
El horizonte desprestigiado
se retiró, se acercó, cambió todo

y todo para que entrara yo:
abajo, arriba, ejido, centro y alrededor.
¿Dónde pasó cada cosa, dónde todo
sucedió? ¿Infancia, juventud, virtud, error?

I

Turning error into virtue,
I'm where my head used to be, seeing all
as far as my eyes could see,
because she—not I—never got lost:

glimpsed in the darkness
of the tunnel, up ahead, one could think
—turning virtue into truth—that the head
was all the occurrence of the light.

And she occurred while I
inside my body did lock myself,
turning each organ into my house:
west or eastward all was windowless,

a happy city uncentered
in the grid of the occasion.
The discredited horizon
withdrew, approached, changed all

and all so enter I could:
down, up, common land, center and surroundings.
Where did each thing happen, where did it all
occur? Childhood, youth, virtue, error?

El tiempo fue quien pasó: salió, subió,
se puso y terminó. Aunque poco, no del todo
definido, el mundo —cabeza y cuerpo—
cobró la forma del contenido,
                              agrandó la o del yo.

Time is who passed: went out, rose,
imposed itself and ended. Although a bit, not all
defined, the world—head and body—
took on the form of the content,
                       expanded the eye of the I.

Trato de Usted a Yo

que según Gertrude no envejece
como me ha pasado a mí.
Toda una vida en el mismo cuerpo,
de un siglo a otro más harapiento,
que Usted, Stein donde esté,
no deja de negar. Soy a Usted
lo que Su Ideal es a mí. Un salón
donde a Usted se lo oye retumbar:
esta lengua está para decirte
que está diciéndote que es esta
y que de una buena vez la escribas.

(Gertrude Stein)

TREATING I AS YOU

which according to Gertrude doesn't grow old
unlike what has happened to me.
A whole life in the same body,
from one century to the next more ragged,
which You, wherever Stein may be,
won't stop denying. I am to You
what Your Ideal is to me. A hall
where the You is heard to reverberate:
this tongue is here to tell you
that it's telling you that this is it
get on with it and write it.

(Gertrude Stein)

La rama de cerezo ornamental,

en su vaso de vidrio verde, pasa a llamarse Jaime
en cuanto traspone la puerta de mi casa.
Jaime me recuerda eso que se pierde

y se quiere celebrar brindando por la vida.
Aun desnuda, enjuta y nervuda,
nerviosa, la rama de cerezo exuda

esa cosa de perenne capullo
que evoca el manto real. Y de hecho es suyo.
El rey no está desnudo, tan sólo lo parece

por pura terquedad. Esa rama despojada
y flaca aloja todas sus flaquezas,
que le permiten alardes y generosidad.

Dará un capullo más, su forma de amistad,
hasta que la reemplace otra rama de cerezo
    ornamental,
con apariencia más joven y casi igual,

que pasa a llamarse Jaime en cuanto traspone
la puerta de mi casa, se zambulle en el vaso
de vidrio verde y me recuerda eso que se pierde.

THE BRANCH OF THE ORNAMENTAL CHERRY TREE,

in its green glass, will be called Jaime
when it crosses the door of my house.
Jaime reminds me of what has been lost

and one means to celebrate when toasting life.
Even nude, shriveled and nervous,
sinewy, the branch of the cherry tree exudes

that thing like a perennial bud
that evokes the regal mantle. From one mud.
The king is not nude, he only appears to be

from pure stubbornness. That branch, stripped
and thin houses all its thinness,
allowing it displays and generosity.

It will give one more bud, its form friendly
until replaced by another branch of the ornamental
    cherry tree,
with a younger appearance the same quite nearly,

that will be called Jaime as soon as it crosses
the door of my house, plunges in the green
glass and reminds me of what has been lost.

Manuel

               en sus *Paraísos desplegados*

Eso que entra por tus ojos y sale de tus manos
tiene fe de bautismo en nuevo mundo;
eso —el altísimo verde de los árboles,
la rastrera sensación de la maleza
o la comunión estancada de las aguas—
ganó ciudadanía, un distinto estatuto de paisaje.

Cada estandarte tuyo señaliza un mundo
abriendo una senda entre los árboles,
convirtiendo el sotobosque de maleza
en patrones intrincados como dedos de las manos.
¿Te dejará entrar en el paisaje
el mesopotámico antojo de las aguas?

En las barrancas de Entre Ríos, en el paisaje
que es un monte surcado por las aguas
y da miedo la certeza que se esconde en la maleza
—la yarará que infunde pánico y cautela—, los árboles
son tótems protectores, puntales de este mundo
donde la naturaleza cedió al fin lugar para tus manos.

Y bajo el techo de las copas de los árboles,

Manuel

                                        in his *Pop-up Paradises*

What enters your eyes and comes out from your hands
has a baptismal certificate in new world;
this—the very tall green of the trees,
the crawling sensation of the weeds
or the stagnant communion of the waters—
has gained citizenship, a different statute of landscape.

Each one of your banners signals a world
a path opening among the trees,
turning the underbrush of weeds
into patterns intricate as the digits of hands.
Will you be allowed in the landscape
by the Mesopotamian whim of the waters?

Along the ridges of Entre Ríos, in the landscape
that is hillsides ploughed by the waters
and the frightening certainty hidden in the weeds
—the yarará that instills panic and caution—the trees
are protective totems, supports from this world
where nature has finally yielded a place for your hands.

And under the crowns of the trees,

sacerdotes de una teología de la maleza
donde Pan camina aún sobre las aguas,
entrás con botas y con guantes, pies y manos
dos corazas contra el horror que aguarda en el paisaje,
un artificio urbano capaz de crear un mundo en otro
    mundo,

una síntesis que respeta la maleza,
su belleza escondida en el paisaje
y que, colgada de los brazos de los árboles
es belleza puesta fuera, muestra del mundo
que vive en tu interior y fluye al ritmo de las aguas,
al unísono con el líquido pulso de tus manos.

Aunque en el cañadón, cuando se estancan las aguas
te dan miedo: allí crece de todo, y arman un paisaje
de corrupción, inmundo, sin siquiera ensuciarse las
    manos.
El miedo, Manuel, es el arma más elegante del mundo:
esa brisa que ondula tu colorida cúpula colgada de los
    árboles,
agita al mismo tiempo, dulce y ominosa, las púas de
    la maleza.

Pero, en guerra y sumisión, traspusiste la maleza y
    fluiste con las aguas.

priests from a theology of weeds
where Pan still walks on the waters,
you enter with boots and gloves, feet and hands
two breastplates against the horror waiting in the
    landscape,
an urban artifice able to create a world in another
    world,

a synthesis that respects the weeds,
its beauty hidden in the landscape
and that, hanging from the arms of the trees
is beauty outward turned, a show of the world
that lives in your interior and flows to the rhythm of
    the waters,
in unison with the liquid pulse of your hands.

Even though in the ravine, when there's stagnant waters
they frighten you: there it all grows, and builds a
    landscape
of corruption, unclean, without even dirtying their
    hands.
Fear, Manuel, is the most elegant weapon in the world:
that breeze that undulates your colorful cupola hanging
    from the trees,
shakes, at the same time, sweet and ominous, the
    barbs of the weeds.

Nunca pensé que en medio de los árboles me darías
   otro paisaje,
asediado por tus ojos, salido de tus manos,
   contradiciendo el mundo.

But in war and in submission, you transposed the
 weeds and flowed with the waters.
I never thought that in the middle of the trees you'd
 give me another landscape,
besieged by your eyes, come out from your hands,
 contradicting the world.

Coda

Y tu mundo nuevo insiste
en lo que en este mundo nadie nunca quiso:
que el Infierno existe en todo Paraíso.

Este poema formó parte de la instalación Paraísos desplegados, *del artista Manuel Ameztoy, que se exhibió entre mayo y julio de 2012 en el Faena Art Center, Buenos Aires.*

CODA

And your new world insists
on what in this world no one ever desired:
that Hell exists in every Paradise.

This poem formed part of the Pop-Up Paradises *installation by the artist Manuel Ameztoy, exhibited between May and July of 2012 at the Faena Art Center in Buenos Aires, Argentina.*

¿SERÁ LA AUTOBIOGRAFÍA

el arrepentimiento del egoísmo? Iris Murdoch puso esa pregunta en boca
de un personaje de sus novelas, yo la convertí en mi abismo. Según he descubierto,
lo vivido noche y día que la escritura pretende rescatar, la gramática que ordena
que una misma se ordene en su tic-tac, que entre en su reflejo y vaya más allá
—donde no hay signos conocidos, y cada gesto resabido, cada tropo,
ya no presta más servicio— deja en suspenso el egoísmo, desconcierta el vicio del yo, permite atisbar lo que no es yo, que ya no aterra. El egoísmo como equivocación,
como instrumento del ensayo y el error —más del error que del ensayo, porque lo hecho hecho está—, es el motor, de mí y de la poesía. Mi egoísmo se llama Iris,
en honor a su descubridora, que lo sacó a la luz, detallado y entero,
en cada verso que yo escribía, y desde entonces me acompaña en cada ensayo
de arrepentimiento, a toda hora. A toda hora ensayo, y a toda hora Iris, fortalecida
en mi obstinación, me ocupa como una palidez.

Could Autobiography

be the regret of selfishness? Iris Murdoch had this
    question come from the mouth
of a character in one of her novels, I turned it into my
    abyss. As I have discovered,
what you live night and day that writing seeks to rescue,
    the grammar that orders
that you order yourself in your tic-tac, that you enter
    your reflection and go beyond
—where there are no familiar signs, and each well-
    known gesture, each trope,
no longer offers its services—leaves selfishness in
    suspense, confounds the vice of the I, allows you
    to catch sight of what is not I, what no longer
    terrifies. Selfishness as equivocation,
an instrument of trial and error—more of error than
    of trial, because what is done is done—is the
    engine, of me and poetry. My selfishness is called
    Iris,
in honor of she who discovered and brought it into
    the light, detailed and whole,
in every verse that I wrote, accompanying me ever since
    around the clock
in every trial of regret. Around the clock I try, and
    around the clock Iris, strengthened

Así es, al punto que ya no puedo distinguir el
    arrepentimiento del egoísmo del que querría
    arrepentirme, y no sé cual de los dos
me mantiene viva, y me cuesta decidirme. Ay, Iris, ¿y
    si vamos juntas
a zambullirnos en Leteo, sin arrepentirnos de nada
    al día siguiente? ¿No sería laxante para el deseo, y
    excelente para el sincretismo en mi poesía? ¿Y si
    nos enamoramos de nuevo, si resucitamos algún
    viejo amor que a lo mejor ni estuvo vivo porque
    fue puro egoísmo?
¿No mejoraría mi poesía, su intensidad? ¿No
    mejoraría? No, en verdad, sería lo mismo aunque
    peor. Se llenaría de adjetivos, de la furia de los
    sonidos. Se haría
enrarecida y mentirosa, y yo lamentaría tener que
    llegar a los setenta en ese estado pueril, llena de
    error y de terror a perder, febril, mi amor y mi
    escritura, que casi siempre fueron para mí, egoísta
    como soy, la sola y misma cosa.

in my obstinacy, overtakes me like a pallor. That's
 how it is, to the point that I can no longer
 distinguish regret from the selfishness I'd want to
 regret, and I don't know which of the two
keeps me alive, and it's hard to decide. Oh, Iris, what
 if we go together
and dive into the Lethe, without regretting anything the
 next day? Wouldn't that be a laxative for desire,
 and excellent for the syncretism of my poetry?
 And if we fall in love again, if we revive some old
 love that perhaps was never alive because it was
 pure selfishness?
Wouldn't my poetry improve then, its intensity?
 Wouldn't it improve? No, truly, it would be the
 same but worse. It would become filled with
 adjectives, with the fury of sounds. It would become
rarefied and untruthful, and I would lament having to
 reach seventy in such an infantile state, full of error
 and terrified of losing, feverish, my love and my
 writing, which have almost always been for me,
 selfish as I am, she, one and the same.

Veinte años de mi vida

vuelven embalsados tras el agua clara de tus ojos
y allí nos veo de los veinte a los cuarenta,
en un abuso de autobiografía,

los años de arder y perder algo cada día,
paciente materia de los versos, donde quedó en
    rastrojo
para volver a su cultivo a los sesenta.

¿No será tarde, no será un acto de arrojo,
temerario, reanudar la mutua compañía
a esta edad cuya sintaxis, más honda, segregada y lenta

nos somete a oscilaciones y súbitos antojos
de un calendario con feriados de manías,
viejas compartidas, aunque la vida sea todo lo que
    cuenta?

Los años de arder, por esta facultad que alojo
de nombrar, han recibido el bautismo de María.
Y por más de un motivo la voluntad que alienta

en ese nombre trae una calma nueva y alegría
pese a que el cuerpo consentido, siempre flojo

Twenty Years of my Life

return embalmed behind the clear water of your eyes
and there I see us from age twenty to forty,
in an autobiographical abuse,

the years of burning and losing something in everyday use,
patient matter of verses, where it remained, in ploughed
    demise,
returned to harvest at age sixty.

Is it not too late, is it not a daring guise,
reckless, our mutual company to resume
at this age whose syntax, deeper, separate, and steady

subjects us to oscillations and whimsical desires
of a calendar with its holidays of insanity,
old shared manias, even if life is all, without excuse?

The years of burning, given this faculty that I assume
for naming, have thus been baptized María.
And for more reasons than one the will excised

from within that name brings new calm and felicity
despite how the pampered body, always loose
of spirit and advancing blindly,

de espíritu y avanzando a tientas,

se rebele, haciéndose notar, y la desmienta.
Pero digo calma somos, no cenizas: palabras al rojo,
como risas, caldean aún la noche más oscura y la más fría.

(Lelé Santilli, María Moreno)

rebels, makes itself known, betrays the new tranquility.
But calm we are, I say, not ashes: words that burn red,
    impute
like laughter, warming us even in the darkest and
    coldest of night.

(Lelé Santilli, María Moreno)

Con Olvido

Que esto que asimilo de tus versos a mi lengua
—la fijeza de la foto, el jirón de pura realidad,
la neta percepción que capta palabras sin más dueño
   que él o ella—
permanezca en mí como si fuera la medida
de la vida —canícula o helada— y de todas las cosas
donde la muerte siempreviva no cede su lugar.

Que en mí queden arraigadas esas cosas
que llevan para mí tu nombre en nuestra lengua:
árboles y pájaros buenos de mirar, aquí y ahora en
   todas las medidas.
Que las formas que son para la vida o los más agudos
   riesgos de ella
—seres y afectos empujándose, el concentrado de su
   cruda realidad—
leyéndote me ocupen por entero, dejándole a la
   muerte su lugar.

El paisaje, por ejemplo, esa realidad
donde somos cada uno simplemente él o ella,
la cara cuando estamos solos, una naturaleza común
   cuya medida

With Olvido

May this that I assimilate from your verses into my
    tongue
—the firmness of the photo, the shred of pure reality,
the clear perception that captures words with no
    other owner than he or she—
remain in me as if it were the measure
of life—canicular or frozen—and of all things
where the liveforever death yields not its place.

May those things remain rooted in me
that carry your name for me in our tongue:
trees and birds good for the eyes, here and now in all
    measures.
May the forms which are made for life or the sharpest
    risks therein
—beings and affections pushing each other, the
    concentrate of its raw reality—
reading you occupy me entirely, leaving death to its
    place.

The landscape, for example, that reality
where each of us is simply he or she,
our face when we're alone, a common nature the
    measure of which

excede con creces el tamaño —que hay o falta— de las
  cosas,
tiene alma —una gran luz— concentrada en esa lengua
hablada en tus poemas, insignias personales de tiempo
  y de lugar.

La espuma ultramarina de tus versos es rocío que cala
  mi lugar.
Así cuando decís: cuando se dice amor ¿quiere decir
  medida?,
o cada una de sus bocas dijo yo, me quedo pensando si
  ser en cada cosa
querrá decir vida, cualquier nada que alimente, la más
  extrema realidad,
y yo tan sólo arena movediza, la mera variante de una
  lengua
que aunque deje de ser yo nunca dejará de ser ella.

Entre quererme y no, me refugio y medro en ella,
y en cada crisis de dolor que exuda realidad
—la intensidad de lo que no corresponde, dirías en mi
  lugar—,
tus versos dan cimiento, gestos lentos, la vacua medida
incalculable de soledad que acopia toda cosa
que queda sin decir, en la punta de la lengua.

exceeds in spades the size—there or missing—of things,
has a soul—a large light—concentrated in that tongue
spoken in your poems, personal insignias of time and
    of place.

The overseas foam of your verses is dew that seeps
    through my place.
Thus when you say: when one says love, is one saying
    measure?
Or each of their mouths said I, I'm left thinking if
    being in each thing
might mean life, any nothingness that may nourish
    us, the most extreme reality,
and I but shifting sand, the mere variant of a tongue
that may stop being I but will never stop being her.

Between loving myself and not, I take refuge and
    flourish in her,
and in each crisis of pain that exudes reality
—the intensity of which doesn't correspond, you'd say
    in my place—
your verses lay the foundation, slow gestures, the
    incalculable measure,
vacuous, of loneliness that gathers everything
left unsaid on the tip of the tongue.

Pero nada queda en la punta de la lengua:
abro al azar un libro tuyo y de la página salta realidad
como si fuera la más evidente de las cosas
de la vida: a los enfermos e impedidos, dice en ella,
diles ea, solos estáis. Como si pudieras ponerte en mi lugar,
como si de este dolor conocieras la medida.

La lengua, raíz de los afectos, casa compartida, es la
    medida
en que las cosas cobran realidad, y en ella tus versos,
vida vivida, vida de tu vida y de la mía, que se pueda,
    que se abra su lugar.

(Olvido García Valdés)

But nothing stays on the tip of the tongue:
I open at random a book of yours and from the page
    jumps reality
as if it were the most evident of things
from life: to the sick and the disabled, it says there,
say hey, thou art alone. As if you could take my place,
as if of this pain you knew the measure.

The tongue, root of affections, shared house, is the
    measure
in which things come into reality, and in it your verses,
lived life, life of your life and of mine, may it be so,
    may it open its place.

(Olvido García Valdés)

JAMES FENTON,

un poeta amigo mío, inglés,
me enseñó la eficacia del verso.

Traduciéndolo, aprendí que lo que es
se puede expresar, idioma terso,

con altura y de manera inteligible,
o bien puede inventarse un lenguaje

que transmita sentimientos y un bagaje
de alternativas, otro mundo posible.

Gracias, James, por tus caprichos sensibles,
por la música cargada de significado

de tus poemas. Traducirlos fue casi imposible.
El casi es lo que aprendí, y agradezco el resultado.

JAMES FENTON,

a poet, friend of mine, English,
taught me the efficacy of verses.

Translating him, I learned that what is
can be expressed, sleek words,

elevated and in a way that's intelligible,
or you can invent a language

that transmits feelings and a baggage
of alternatives, another world that's possible.

Thank you, James, for your whims that are sensible,
for the music loaded, in your poems,

with meaning. Translating them was almost impossible.
The almost is what I learned, and am grateful for the
    outcomes.

INTERIOR LANDSCAPE
EL PAISAJE INTERIOR

and if my body is still the soft part of the mountain
I will know
that I am not yet the mountain.

y si mi cuerpo sigue siendo la parte blanda de la montaña
sabré
que aún no soy la montaña.

José Watanabe

Madrugada y viento
bajo el cielo lento
y esta luz también
para mí:
lentamente ir
de acá para allá
sin adjetivos
y con dificultad,
hablar por teléfono
—nada personal—
ejercitarse y pensar
en palabras que acontezcan además
fuera de mí, ser un ejército,
cocinar papas
zapallos y guisantes
y comérselos como un festín.

Las palabras, está comprobado,
no llegan a su fin.

De acá para allá todavía
cuando el día ostenta
su cielo vespertino
en camino a la oscuridad
y las palabras con su recuento
—inválido y a tientas—

Dawn and wind
under the slow sky
and this light also
for me:
slowly going
from here to there
without adjectives
but with difficulty,
speaking on the phone
—nothing personal—
exercising and thinking
in words that also happen
outside of me, be an army,
cook potatoes
squash and peas
eat it like a feast.

Words, it is proven,
do not reach their end.

From here to there still
as the day flaunts
its evening sky
on the way to darkness
and the words with their recounting
—invalid and bumbling—

de lo que pasó y lo que es.
No hacer cuentas.

Sentarse y contar el aliento,
una respiración por vez.
Terminar.

what happened and what is.
Don't add it up.

Sit down and count your breathing
one gulp of air at a time.
Finish.

AHORA, más cerca de la tierra,
veo las mismas cosas
pero veo más. Sentarse
para evitar la distracción,
y la ilusión retrocede.
Puede menos y sé más
aunque no sepa nada nuevo:
¿seguramente no habrá?
propone el yo
que no alcanzó el desapego.

Sentarse y desconfiar.

Now, closer to the earth,
I see the same things
but I see more. Sit down
to avoid distraction,
and illusion recedes.
You can do less but be more
without knowing anything new:
there probably isn't?
proposes the I
that never reached detachment.

Sit down and mistrust.

La casa se convirtió en mi madre,
un caparazón
que me cuida y me encarcela.

La palabra mamá
centellea, deslumbra y ciega.

Y yo acá
chocándome con las cosas
por ir de acá para allá.
Palabras es lo que no eran.

Mamá. Mamá.
La hija que ya es abuela.
Unas pocas sílabas rielan
como el mar.

Sentarse y a nadar.

THE HOUSE became my mother,
a shell
that takes care of and imprisons me.

The word mama
flashes, dazzles, and blinds.

And here I am
running into things
as I go from here to there.
Words is what they were not.

Mama. Mama.
The daughter already a grandmother.
A few syllables shimmer
like the sea.

Sit down and start to swim.

No sé por qué
veo más. Esta
atmósfera sedente
no atrapó mi cabeza
obstinada en ganar altura,
acontecer allá arriba,
gobernar. El paisaje
interior, Manley Hopkins,
sangra por la herida,
sutura el yo. La verdad,
la virtud, la ilusión, son leudantes
de la vida. Ir adelante, arriba,
avanzar hacia allá, tener pensamientos,
evitar los adjetivos. No calificar.

Sentarse y saber dominar.

I DON'T know why
I see more. This
sedentary atmosphere
did not trap my head
obstinate to gain height,
to occur up there,
to govern. The interior
landscape, Manley Hopkins,
bleeds out the wound,
sutures the I. Truth,
virtue, illusion, are leaveners
of life. Go forward, upward,
move over there, have thoughts,
avoid adjectives. Don't qualify.

Sit down and know how to control.

Saber dominarse.
Sentada con la cabeza
en las nubes, contemplar
cómo pasan, altas, feas,
disciplinar las ideas,
las palabras un ejército
que va de acá para allá
bajo órdenes del yo
da pelea, le va mal.

Sentarse y capitular.

KNOW to self-control.
Sitting with my head
in the clouds, contemplating
their passing, high, ugly,
discipline ideas,
words an army
going from here to there
under orders from the I
fights back, not going well.

Sit down and capitulate.

SALIR de Mamá al mundo
madre pública y social.
Escucho, hablo, me hablás.
Empiezan los adjetivos:
un buen recital de poesía,
gran lectura, interesante
estructura, cosas
que hacen pensar.
El yo pasa al subjuntivo:
que yo sea tu enemigo.

Sentarse y dejar pasar.

Exit from Mama to the world
public and social mother.
I listen, I speak, you speak to me.
The adjectives begin:
a good poetry recital,
great reading, interesting
structure, things
that make you think.
The I goes onto the subjunctive:
that I may become your enemy.

Sit down and let it go.

CAER de culo
irse al traste
y terminar sentada
sobre la palabra culo,
chocarse con la realidad.
Con dos sílabas basta:
sea culo, dolor, estar.

Sentarse y que te vengan
a levantar.

FALL on your ass
go to pot
and end up sitting
on the word ass
crash against reality.
One syllable is enough:
be it ass, pain, stuck.

Sit down and let them come
to pick you up.

La cabeza arriba
abajo brazos
manos y pies, mi trabajo,
el tronco con su cintura
una cultura del sur,
las rodillas, las caderas
dedos, pelo, uñas, vísceras, encías.

Sentarse y en una lista
ultimar la biografía.

THE HEAD above
below arms
hands and feet, my work,
the trunk with its waist
a culture from the south,
the knees, the hips
fingers, hair, nails, viscera, gums.

Sit down and in a list
finish off the biography.

Vas a verme,
me ves
y no sé lo que verás.
Sea lo que sea,
más allá de lo que veas
siempre estoy yo además.

Sentarse y dejar entrar.

You're going to see me,
you see me
and I don't know what you'll see.
Whatever it may be,
beyond what you see
I am always here additionally.

Sit down and open up.

Bajó mi centro
de gravedad. Ahora gravito más
más cercana
a la raíz que al capullo
del cerezo ornamental,
(se está floreando una rama
en el florero que era de mi papá),
al limonero y su tronco
que a los limones que da
(en el patio de mi hijo
cunde verde y amarillo).

Busco cosas para poder decirlo:
¿Se encogió mi yo, perdió brillo?
¿Dejó de actuar, Iris Murdoch,
el teatro de los sentimientos
porque se acortó el intervalo
entre pies y coronilla?
¿Ahora siente de verdad,
y yo no miento?

Sentarse y no contestar.

IT'S LOWERED, my center
of gravity. Now I gravitate more
quite closer
to the root than the bud
of the ornamental cherry tree,
(a branch flowering
in the vase that was once my papa's),
to the lemon tree and its trunk
than to the lemons it produces
(in my son's patio
green and yellow spreads).

I search for things so I may say it:
Has my I shrunk, has it lost its glow?
Has the theater of sentiments
stopped performing, Iris Murdoch,
because the interval has been shortened
between feet and crown?
Does it truly feel now,
and I'm not lying?

Sit down and answer not.

Cómo empieza una casa
Mamá, cómo termina
tan chica como esta.
Cómo fue que seguí a esa
mujer cómo fue que me siguió
para después poder plantarme.
Soy esa semilla.
Pero la casa es mía
y las palabras que tiene adentro.
Mamá. Mamá. Yo. Hoy.
Una casa tan chica como esta,
cosas que no supe descartar
o regalar y palabras que la atestan.
No tienen fin en una casa
tan chica como esta.

Sentarse y aquí plantada
soltar hojas y nuevas ramas.

How does a house begin
Mama, how does it end up
being as small as this one.
How did I come to follow that
woman how did she come to follow me
only to later leave me planted.
I am that seed.
But the house is mine
and the words it has inside.
Mama. Mama. I. Today.
A house as small as this one,
things I didn't know how to discard
or give away and words that attest to it.
There is no end to them in a house
as small as this one.

Sit down and planted here
release branches and new leaves.

Bajo y voy al lado
 o voy enfrente. Cadente
el ámbito del sol
por el que voy de acá para allá.
Al kiosco y luego al bar.
Ya salí, ya volví,
el ascensor me sube
pero no me hace más alta.
Pura promesa, pienso
en todo lo que falta
y en esta casa tan chica
que es mi casa de las palabras.

Sobre la mesa,
un limón se vanagloria
ofreciendo el sol
que escasea en la vereda,
la palabra limón,
tal como mi maestro demostró,
rima con dragón,
sobre todo si es dorado
y parece un lanzallamas.
¿Será que el mundo rima
demasiado?¿Tendré
que irme por las ramas?

Sentarse y ponderar.

I HEAD DOWN and go next door
or across the street. Cadent
the field of the sun
that I cross from here to there.
To the kiosk and then the café.
I've gone out, I'm back,
the elevator lifts me
but doesn't make me taller.
Pure promise, I think
in everything that's missing
and in this such-small house
that is my house of words.

On the table,
a lemon boasts
providing the sun
that's scarce on the sidewalk,
the word lemon,
as my teacher demonstrated,
rhymes with dragon,
especially if it's golden
and looks like a flamethrower.
Does the world rhyme
too much? Should I
allow myself to branch off?

Sit down and ponder.

Es la infatuación:
el amor al amor,
el odio al odio,
vuelven las cosas opacas
y las palabras flacas,
ilusión que no hace sombra.

El amor solo y el odio claramente
vuelven las cosas transparentes
pero con sombra propia
y las palabras fibrosas
no son copia de la cosa
donde encarna el yo.

Te amo y odio,
sí y no,
y desde hace tantos años
que el daño está claro:
somos yo y yo y vos.

Sentarse y aprender el dos.

It is infatuation:
the love of love,
the hate of hate,
turn things opaque
and thin the words,
illusion that casts no shadow.

Love by itself and hate clearly
turn things transparent
but with their own shadow
and words fibrous
of the thing are not a copy
where the I is embodied.

I love and hate you,
yes and no,
and for so many years
that the damage is clear:
we are I and I and you.

Sit down and learn the two.

Dichoso aquél, Safo querida,
que antes de morir puede decir con alegría
gasté todo el tesoro de los celos.

Sentarse a ser pobre.
Tener miedo.

FORTUNATE is the one, dear Sappho,
who can before dying say with joy
I have spent the entire treasure of jealousy.

Sit down to be poor.
Be afraid.

Si me das por muerta,
pese al miedo sigo aquí sentada.
No se diga de alguien que es feliz
si no está muerto todavía,
dice el último coro del Edipo,
como si vivo el animal del ser
sólo pudiera ver
las cosas a su altura.
Feliz queda más alto
o tal vez muy por debajo.

Pero si me das por muerta
se abre la puerta,
y cuánto te quería,
cuánto trabajo.

Es de día
y subo a oscuras,
la tiniebla opaca lo que se termina.
Aun infeliz,
ver la raíz,
intuir la luz al final del túnel.

Sentarse y buscar la salida.

If you take me for dead,
despite the fear I'm still sitting here.
Don't say that someone's happy
if they're not dead yet,
says the last chorus in Oedipus,
as if alive the animal of to be
was only able to see
things at their height.
Happy lies even higher
or perhaps much further below.

But if you take me for dead
the door opens ahead,
and how I loved you,
how much work.

It's daytime
and I go up sightless,
darkness makes opaque what ends.
Yet unhappy,
see the root,
intuit the light at the end of the tunnel.

Sit down and look for the exit.

El único mortal feliz,
dice Sófocles,
es el mortal muerto.

Sentarse a pensar
y ser quien piensa
que es amor y no una ofensa
tu manera de desearme
desaparición,
felicidad auténtica.

The only happy mortal,
Sophocles says,
is a dead mortal.

Sit down to think
and be she who thinks
that it's love and not an affront
your way of desiring me
disappearance,
authentic happiness.

Las emociones del medio,
dice Iris Murdoch,
se actúan. Sólo son de verdad
las del tope o de la base
de la personalidad,
las de verdad extremas,
un huerto personal
lleno de especies monstruosas,
(árboles que se van haciendo árboles,
todas sus orugas se van haciendo hojas,
dice García Valdés), y ahí se quedan
testigos invisibles ominosos
resultados de que viví
sobreactué y estoy arrepentida
de mi incursión mendaz en el teatro.

Sentarse y al último acto.

THE EMOTIONS in the middle,
Iris Murdoch says,
are an act. Only true are
the ones at the top or the bottom
of one's personality,
the ones truly at the extremes,
a personal orchard
full of monstrous species,
(trees that become trees,
all their caterpillars become leaves,
García Valdés says), and there they stay
invisible ominous witnesses
results that I have lived
overacted and I regret
my mendacious incursion into the theater.

Sit down for the last act.

UN TEMBLOR
que la escala de Richter
no registra: no fui
al funeral de mi hermano,
nunca volveré a hacerlo.
Seguro recordaba
tanto a su madre
como un caballo de ocho años,
dice Shakespeare de alguien,
creo que en Coriolano.
Si no, tal vez
no hubiera hecho mutis
dejándome hija única tardíamente
aquí sentada y con Mamá
por todos lados.

A TREMOR
that the Richter scale
does not register: I did not go
to my brother's funeral,
I will never do that again.
He surely remembered
his mother as much
as an eight-year-old horse,
Shakespeare says about someone,
I believe in Coriolanus.
If not, maybe
he wouldn't have gone mutis
belatedly leaving me an only daughter
sitting here and with Mama
everywhere.

Dichosa aquella, Witold Gombrowicz,
que en el mes diez
cumple sesenta
el día siete
y se alegra de haber llegado
y de poder hacer la cuenta.

Es el Día del Perdón,
buena ocasión
para que toda mi familia judía
me ofrezca absolución
porque jamás les hice nada
ni pedí. Aquí
sentada con mi propio Libro de Números,
largo y asimétrico como el húmero,
ni levita ni coanita,
advierto que soy todo un pueblo
si tengo en cuenta el dolor, mis lecturas aplicadas
y yo. El resultado de censar mi vida
trae esta frase pulida,
y Gombrowicz tiene razón:
"No hay horror que no consiga amor".
No, no hay, y ¡ay!
tampoco hay nada mejor.

Sentarse y aun a oscuras
proseguir con la lectura.

FORTUNATE is she, Witold Gombrowicz,
who on the tenth month
turns sixty
on the seventh day
and is happy to have arrived
and be able to add it all up.

It's the Day of Atonement,
good occasion
for my entire Jewish family
to offer me absolution
since I never did anything to them
nor asked. Here
sitting with my own Book of Numbers,
long and asymmetric as the humerus,
neither Leviim nor Kohanim,
I note that I'm an entire people
if I take into account the pain, my applied readings
and I. The result of censusing my life
brings this polished phrase,
and Gombrowicz is right:
"There is no horror that does not lead to love."
No, there is not, and oh!
there is also nothing better.

Sit down and even in darkness
continue with the reading.

INTIMATE BESTIARY
BESTIARIO ÍNTIMO

Gato en retrato

Si se pierde el momento
de empezar
        se empieza
en cualquier lado: aunque
se pierda
        el gato
está ganado. Y no se espera.

Ni siquiera
        el gato espera al gato.

El gato es solo
y eso le permite
        inventarse
sus pasiones. Su riesgo
es saber
        y de antemano
que nadie lo querrá
como querría.
        Y ésta:
"Gato en el mundo,
poco profundo",
        su sentencia.

CAT IN PORTRAIT

If one misses the starting
point
        one starts
anywhere: even if
one loses
        the cat
is won. And no one waits.

Not even
        the cat waits for the cat.

The cat's alone
and that allows it
        to invent itself
its passions. Its risk
is to know
        and beforehand
that no one will want it
like it would want.
        And this:
"Cat even asleep,
not so deep,"
        its sentence.

Siendo leve,
el gato es. Se sueña
con gatos
   cuando uno
se sale de sí mismo. El gato
rara vez
cabe en el gato.

       Está
autorizado al equilibrio
y condenado
          por lo mismo
a sitios relativos:
   sube
y no se asciende, baja
y no se hunde.

El único lugar del gato
es donde
el gato estuvo.

       Según
mi amiga,
       en Roma
hay siempre el mismo
       gato.

Being slight,
the cat is. One dreams
with cats
when one
is outside oneself. The cat
rarely
fits in the cat.

              It is
authorized for equilibrium
and condemned
              for the same
to relative sites:
   it climbs
but does not rise, it descends
but does not sink.

The cat's only place
is where
the cat was.

              According
to my friend,
            in Rome
it's always the same
      cat.

Se renuevan
        sin embargo
los gatos de París. Y hay
más de uno siempre a un tris
de ser feliz
        aquí.

El aquí
es el conflicto del gato.
De donde mira
        ve
que el mundo gira
y se marea. Gato mareado,
gato agotado. Lo pierde
lo relativo
   y ni lo salva
saber que está ganado
aunque perdido.

They're renewed
                however
the cats in Paris. And there's
always more than one that's snappy
and quite happy
                here, see.

The here
is the cat's conflict.
Wherever it looks from
                it sees
that the world turns
and it gets dazed. Dazed cat,
tired cat. It's lost by
what's relative
    and it's not even saved
when it knows it has won
although lost.

La morena o
la soberanía no es una mascota doméstica

Vive voraz en el agua
la morena carnicera
de profundidad,
                    pequeña
si se compara
con ballena o tiburón —metro y medio
de extensión en el mar Mediterráneo.
Pez foráneo que no crece,
                    acá,
en el Paraná, sin excepción la morena
a la anguila se parece
                    que se parece
a la víbora: si no se arrastra,
es que nada. Toda
una ese carnívora, sinuosamente
garganta, traga porque querría
mostrar que no sabría vivir
de otra manera. Si espera
ondula ese cuerpo que ella finge
no tener: por mujer, pura-cabeza
y de mula, está esperando una presa
que la haga suya y la deje,
                    además,

The Moray or
Sovereignty is Not a Domestic Pet

   Voracious she lives in the water
the moray a butcher
of the depths,

                little

if compared
with whale or shark—meter and a half
in length in the Mediterranean Sea.
Foreign fish that doesn't grow,

                        here,

in the Paraná River, without exception the moray
resembles the eel

                  that resembles

the snake: if not slithering,
she's swimming. All a
carnivorous S, a sinuous
throat, she swallows as if
to show she wouldn't know how to live
any other way. If waiting
she curls up that body she pretends
not to have: as woman, head always
and as mule, she's waiting for preys
to make it hers and allow her,

                        besides,

hacer. Es difícil ser un pez,
$\qquad\qquad\qquad$ pero se es
lo que se es, y en la duda
se está en paz:
$\qquad\qquad$ una
centella con ojos
de criatura o creación, preferentemente
$\qquad\qquad\qquad\qquad\qquad$ sola
tras el cristal del acuario, es ella
sin ser fatal. A diario
hay que hacer cola
por verla en exposición.

to do her thing. It is hard to be a fish,

                                              but it is

what it is, and if in doubt
it is in peace:

              a

flash with eyes
of a creature or creation, preferentially

                                  alone

behind the glass of the aquarium, it is her
without being fatal. Daily
you have to wait in line
to see her in exhibition.

Perros de mi familia

No se la pasan
ladrándole a la luna llena. Se sientan
a la mesa de la cena, con perros amigos,
y conversan sobre ella, hacen listas.
Perros artistas,
lo digo porque los he visto.

Cuatro patas, cola y afectivo:
en esencia, un sustantivo colectivo
que sin embargo anda solo: cada perro
es EL perro.
     Y aunque
acepte la vigilia de ser fiel,
lo es primero a sí mismo,
ni al paseo ni al encierro.
     De a dos,
de a tres, de a diez,
todos son un solo perro,
    convencido
de que el mundo no es lugar
hecho por y solamente
    para perros:

¡tantas cosas que arreglar,
tanta fealdad inminente!

DOGS IN MY FAMILY

They don't stand around
barking at the full moon. They sit
at the dinner table, with their dog friends,
and talk about her, they make lists.
Dog artistes
I say this because I've seen them.

Four legs, tail, and affective:
in essence, a noun that's collective
that nonetheless runs alone: every dog
is THE dog.
         And although
it accepts the vigil of being loyal,
it is so first of all to itself,
not to going out or staying in.
         Two at a time,
or three, or ten,
they're all a single dog,
         convinced
that the world is not a place
made by and solely
         for dogs:

so many things to fix,
so much imminent ugliness!

A veces se impone hablar,
y no siempre decir ¡Guau!
　　　　Como sea,
es muy capaz de cantarle las cuarenta
prácticamente a cualquiera
　　　　　y hasta dialogar
con ballenas —véase si no
"perros cantores de Nueva Guinea"—,
según lo sienta y sea feliz.

El amor lo hace feliz
y perseguirse la cola,
ser un círculo perfecto
en sagrado frenesí —"Para empezar",
le dijo el gato a Alicia,
"los perros no están locos". Y ella:
"Supongo que sí"—.

　　　　Lo digo
porque yo misma los vi:
　　　　　perros de mi familia
en furiosa actividad
—justicia, belleza, verdad—
imaginando otros mundos
que, como éste,
también habría que cambiar.

Sometimes talking is imposed
and not always saying Woof!
                In any case,
it's very much able to tell off
practically anyone
           and even to dialogue
with whales—if not, see
"New Guinea singing dogs"—
as it feels and is happy.

Love makes it happy
and chasing its own tale,
being a perfect circle
in sacred frenzy—"To begin with,"
the cat said to Alice,
"a dog's not mad." And she:
"I suppose so."

              I say this
for I myself have seen them:
        dogs in my family
in furious activity
—justice, beauty, truth—
imagining other worlds
which, like this one,
also should be changed.

Si alguien querría ser una tortuga

      sería yo:
hacer de una sección cónica
mi propia sede prehistórica
alojada en la espina dorsal.

Ser tortuga
            tiene algo de ideal:
desde joven luce arrugas
y en sentido literal
se hace mayor con los años
           —a más edad
más tamaño.
             Post-matrimonial,
sin lazos familiares
después de desovar,
igual a todas y cada una,
naturalmente hija de la luna,
            sin embargo
no hay cisma
entre ella misma y sus lares.

Entre tantos avatares,
                para mí
que estoy en mí

If Someone Would Like to be a Turtle

that would be me:
make from a section that's conical
my own headquarters, prehistorical,
lodged in the spinal cord.

Being a turtle
                is somewhat ideal:
sporting wrinkles from youth
and in a sense that's literal
getting older with years
       —the greater the age
the greater the size.
        Post-matrimonial,
without family ties
after laying eggs,
the same with each and every one,
naturally a daughter of the moon,
               and soon
there are no scars
between herself and her lars.

With so many vicissitudes,
             for me
here inside of me

—puro apremio sin molicie—,
poco cuenta que sea lenta
su marcha en la superficie:
          eso
me haría durar
y capaz de entrar al mar,
—que cubre dos tercios del mundo—
sabiendo que si me hundo
gano velocidad.

—pure urgency without blandness—
it matters not that it be low and slow
her march along the surface:
     that
would make me, lastly
perhaps enter the sea
—that covers two thirds of the planet—
knowing that if I plummet
I gain in velocity.

Una hiena en mi vereda

¿Por qué me siguió
esa hiena, le habré dado pena?
Antipático animal,
amable sin embargo
al decir de los etólogos,
la grandísima epicena
fue para mí un trago amargo.

¿De qué se ríe esa mujer,
          esa hiena?
¿De qué se ríe? ¿Es mujer
o hace la escena? ¿La famosa
risa histérica? Si ni siquiera
es de América, ¿estará
desorientada? Vive roja
casi al lado y yo,
que quiero convertirme en nada,
tengo que oír sus consejos
y necias admoniciones:
"en tus condiciones",
dijo en varias ocasiones,
"no podés exigir demasiado.
Pero estoy acá para eso, para que puedas necesitar",
y amagó con darme un beso.

A Hyena on my Sidewalk

Why did that hyena
follow me, did it pity me?
Unpleasant animal,
friendly though
according to the ethologists,
the very great epicene
was a bitter drink for me.

What is that woman laughing at,
                that hyena?
What is she laughing at? Is she a woman
or making a scene? The famous
hysterical laughter? If she's not even
from the Americas, could she be
disoriented? Red she lives
almost next door and I,
who wish to become nothing,
have to listen to her advice
and dumb warnings:
"in your condition,"
she's said on several occasions,
"you can't demand so much.
But that's why I'm here, so you can have needs,"
and she feinted as if to kiss me.

Mi vecina carroñera
tiene paciencia y espera.

Aunque a veces me da pánico,
algo me atrae de este cánido:
pese a que vivo sentada, en franco diminuendo,
parece seguir creyendo,
        —indulgente hiena obscena—
que mi carne vale la pena.

My scavenger neighbor
waits and belabors.

Although sometimes I get panicky,
something about this canine attracts me:
though I live sitting down, frankly in diminishment,
she still thinks to my astonishment,
                —indulgent obscene hyena—
that my flesh is a worthy arena.

CONVERSOS

Incluyo aquí traducciones de poesía que hice durante los últimos años, y que, según considero, ejercieron influencia sobre mi propia escritura.

La serie de poemas que abre esta selección pertenece a *The Interior Landscape* (por casualidad, el mismo título de este libro, que en realidad es mi versión del término *inscape*, acuñado por Gerald Manley Hopkins en el siglo XIX, y que suele traducirse, a mi entender erróneamente, como "esencia"). Se trata de una compilación de poemas de amor del *Kuruntokai*, una de las ocho antologías tamiles clásicas, atribuidas a los tres primeros siglos d. C. *The Interior Landscape* fue compilado y traducido al inglés por A.K. Ramanujan (1929–1993), un especialista en literatura india que escribió tanto en inglés como en lengua kannada. Fue poeta, académico, filólogo y traductor. Sus investigaciones académicas se desarrollaron en cinco lenguas: tamil, kannada, telugu, sánscrito e inglés. Enseñó en universidades de Estados Unidos, y fue muy respetado por su labor como traductor y por su propia poética. Sus traducciones del tamil al inglés son consideradas clásicos. La antología en inglés está acompañada por un minucioso epílogo donde Ramanujan pone en contexto los poemas para mejor comprensión de los lectores occidentales. El librito es una verdadera joya, que debo a la generosidad de Reynaldo Jiménez, quien me

I include here translations of poetry that I did in the last few years and which, in my own estimation, have exercised an influence over my own writing.

The series of poems that opens this selection belongs to *The Interior Landscape* (incidentally, the same title as that of this book, which is in reality my version of the term *inscape*, coined by Gerald Manley Hopkins in the nineteenth century; and which is usually translated into Spanish, erroneously as far as I'm concerned, as "essence.") It is composed of a compilation of love poems from the *Kuruntokai*, one of the eight anthologies of classical Tamil poetry, believed to be from the first century A.C. *The Interior Landscape* was compiled and translated into English by A.K. Ramanujan (1929–1993), a specialist in Indian Literature who wrote in English as well as Kannada. He was a poet, an academic, a philologist, and a translator. His academic research was in five languages: Tamil, Kannada, Telugu, Sanskrit, and English. He taught in universities in the United States, and was very respected for his work as a translator and for his own poetic production. His translations from Tamil into English are considered classics. The anthology in English is accompanied by a detailed epilogue in which Ramanujan contextualizes the poems to improve their comprehension by Western readers. I owe this true gem of a book to the

lo obsequió tras un viaje a la India. Los poemas se presentan como monólogos dramáticos, enunciados por ella, él, la amiga de ella, su madre adoptiva, los que los ven pasar, la concubina, etc.

El resto de los poemas están vertidos directamente del inglés y, salvo Bishop y Lowell, consagrados del panteón de la poesía, pertenecen a poetas vivos. "Tsunami", de James Fenton, es el poema central de un ciclo de canciones cuyo argumento tiene como protagonista a un hombre que sufre con profunda amargura la destrucción de su matrimonio y que en este caso compara su situación con la catástrofe natural, con un grado de musicalidad y lirismo indudablemente *cantabile*. De Kay Ryan admiro su concisión, el juego fónico y la impecable factura y solidez que consigue en sus versos breves, todos ellos rasgos difíciles de reproducir en castellano. Ojalá mis versiones guarden aunque sea una lejana semejanza con las virtudes de los poemas.

generosity of Reynaldo Jiménez, who brought it for me as a gift from a trip to India. The poems appear as dramatic monologues, enunciated by her, him, her friend, her adoptive mother, the ones who see them pass by, the concubine, etc.

The rest of the poems are translated directly from English and, except for the ones by the consecrated Bishop and Lowell, belong to living poets. "Tsunami," by James Fenton, is the central poem of a cycle of songs whose storyline has as its protagonist a man who suffers the destruction of his marriage with deep bitterness and who, in this case, compares his situation with a natural catastrophe, with a degree of musicality and lyricism that is undoubtedly cantabile. Of Kay Ryan I admire the concision, the phonic games, and the impeccable workmanship and solidity she achieves in her short verses—all difficult characteristics to reproduce in Spanish. Hopefully my versions bear at least a distant resemblance to the virtues of the poems.

WHAT SHE SAID

Bigger than earth, certainly,
higher than the sky,
more unfathomable than the waters
is this love for this man

> of the mountain slopes
> where bees make rich honey
> from the flowers of the *kuṟiñci*
> that has such black stalks.

> *Tēvakulattār*
> *Kuṟ 3*

Lo que dijo ella

Más grande que la tierra, por cierto,
más alto que el cielo,
más insondable que las aguas
es este amor por ese hombre

                de las laderas de la montaña
                donde las abejas hacen rica miel
                de las flores del *kuriñci*
                que tiene tallos tan negros.

                        Tēvakulattār
                        Kur 3

WHAT SHE SAID

The still drone of the time
past midnight.
All words put out,
men are sunk into the sweetness
of sleep. Even the far-flung world
has put aside its rages
for sleep.

        Only I
am awake.

Patumaṉār
Kuṟ 6

Lo que dijo ella

Zumba quedo el tiempo
después de medianoche.
Acalladas las palabras,
los hombres se hunden en la dulzura
del sueño. Hasta el vasto mundo
dejó a un lado su furor
para dormir.

              Sólo yo
estoy despierta.

Patumaṉār
Kuṟ 6

WHAT THE PASSERS-BY SAID

This bowman has a warrior's band
on his ankle;
the girl with the bracelets on her arm
has a virgin's anklets
on her tender feet.

    They look like good people.

In these places
the winds beat upon the *vākai* trees
and make the white seedpods rattle
like drums for acrobats
dancing on the tightropes.

Poor things, who could they be?
and what makes them walk
with all the others
through these desert ways
so filled with bamboos?

Perumpatumanār
Kur̲ 7

Los que dijeron los que los vieron pasar

Este arquero lleva una banda de guerrero
en el tobillo;
la joven del brazalete en la muñeca
luce sobre el tierno pie
ajorcas de virgen.

      Parecen buena gente.

En estos parajes
el viento bate
contra los árboles de *vākai*
y hace que las blancas vainas suenen
como los tambores de los acróbatas
que danzan sobre la cuerda floja.

Pobrecitos, ¿quiénes podrán ser?
¿y qué los lleva a caminar
con todos los otros
por estos desiertos parajes
tan llenos de bambúes?

        Perumpatumaṉār
        Kuṟ 7

WHAT THE CONCUBINE SAID

You know he comes from
where the fresh-water sharks in the pools
catch with their mouths
the mangoes as they fall, ripe
from the trees on the edge of the field.

At our place
he talked big.
      Now, back in his own,
when others raise their hands
and feet,
he will raise his too:

like a doll
in a mirror
he will shadow
every last wish
of his son's dear mother.

Ālaṅkuṭi Vaṅkaṉār
Kuṟ 8

Lo que dijo la concubina

Sabes que viene del lugar
donde los tiburones de agua dulce en los estanques
atrapan con la boca
los mangos que caen, maduros,
de los árboles que crecen en el borde del campo.

Entre nosotros
se llenó la boca de palabras altisonantes.
      Ahora, de vuelta con los suyos,
cuando los demás levanten las manos
y los pies,
él también lo hará:

como un títere
en un espejo
será el reflejo
de cada último deseo
de la querida madre de su hijo.

Ālaṅkuṭi Vaṉkaṉār
Kuṟ 8

WHAT THE FOSTER-MOTHER SAID

He had a beautiful war bracelet
and his white spear
had a red tongue
for a blade,
and she had many bangles
on her hand.

Her love has come true
like the infallible word
of the *Kōcars* from the four villages
gathered under the ancient banyan;

as the wedding drums thunder,
and the conch-shell trumpets blare,

her love is made good and true.

Auvaiyār
Kur̲ 15

Lo que dijo la madrina de ella

Él llevaba un bello brazalete de guerra
y su lanza blanca
tenía una lengua roja
como afilada punta
y ella tenía muchos cascabeles
en la mano.

El amor de ella se ha vuelto tan cierto
como la palabra infalible
de los *Kōcars* de las cuatro aldeas
reunidos bajo el viejo baniano;

mientras atruenan los tambores nupciales,
y resuenan estridentes las trompas de caracolas,

su amor se vuelve bueno y cierto.

Auvaiyār
Kur̲ 15

WHAT HE SAID

When love is ripe beyond bearing
and goes to seed,
men will ride even palmyra stems
as if they were horses; will wear on their heads
the reeking cones of the *erukkam* bud
as if they were flowers;
will draw to themselves
the laughter of the streets;

and will do worse.

Pēreyiṉ Muṟuvalār
Kuṟ 17

Lo que dijo él

Cuando el amor madura en exceso
y se vuelve semilla,
los hombres cabalgarán los tallos de palmira
como si fueran caballos, coronarán sus cabezas
con los hediondos conos del fruto del *erukkam*
como si fueran flores; atraerán sobre sí
los chismes de la calle;

y harán cosas peores.

Pēreyiṉ Muṟuvalār
Kuṟ 17

TSUNAMI
James Fenton

This furniture is arrogant. It gives itself airs.
I put away some studio glass and rearrange the chairs
And fill a bowl with bright, unblemished fruit
And place it near the lamp,
Find a green vase and shove some anemones in it.
None of this fools me for a minute.
It hardly even helps to pass the time
But optimism is no crime
And the anemones know what to do
Opening in black and the profoundest blue.

Accommodating flowers:
Cut, crated up, they travel for hours
And come out looking only a little crushed.
And see how quickly they revive!
They are exemplary. They are so blue.
They are too generous to be true.
They almost make you glad to be alive.

I have a world at my command.
I eat alone with the remote in hand.
Night after night, they play the same footage over.
And the wave comes crashing through the tree line

Hitting the palms at coconut height.
You want to say: that can't be right—
The water is out of scale with the trees.
Run it past me again please.

Now here it comes again, the great wave.
Here comes the wave straight through the crown of
    the trees.
And oh, it has taken all I have:
Wife, children, home, all gone,
Gone, sucked back down through the coconut line,
Beyond the sand bar, out over the reef,
Beyond the reach of human strength and grief.

The first thing they knew
The whole of the sea had disappeared from view
So fast it left a beach covered with fish
A miracle upon the shore, something never seen before,
Like the fulfillment of an idiot's wish,
And the children ran down to fill their arms with food
Shouting and laughing at this absurd surprise
And quite unable to hear the cries
Of those who called them back. Then came the wave.

Then came the wave. The fishermen out at sea
Felt only one green force heaving the boat

Which left them all undamaged and afloat.
Yet still they marked the moment by the sun,
Not calibrating in that instant all they had lost—
Wife, children, home, village all gone
With every landmark of their native coast—

Till, caught in a solemn dread for what was theirs,
They steered for the shore
And making landfall, looking each to each,
Dragging their keels up what had once been beach,
They knew themselves a fleet of widowers,
The lucky ones, the absentees,
Alone, alive among the uprooted trees,
Unwelcome to the objects of their love.

TSUNAMI
translated by Mirta Rosenberg

Este mobiliario es arrogante. No para de alardear.
Escondo la cristalería del estudio y cambio sillas de lugar
y lleno un cuenco con frutas coloridas, sin defecto
y lo pongo cerca de la lámpara,
encuentro un jarrón verde y meto adentro
unas anémonas que crean buen efecto.
Nada de esto me engaña ni un momento.
Apenas si me ayuda a lograr que pase el tiempo
pero el optimismo no es un crimen, según siento,
y las anémonas conocen bien su oficio:
abrirse en negro y en azules profundísimos.

Flores indulgentes:
cortadas, envasadas, viajan horas y horas como nada
y reaparecen apenas aplastadas.
¡Y con qué rapidez recobran lozanía!
Son ejemplares. Tan azules en su intensidad.
Son demasiado buenas para ser verdad.
Casi te alegran de seguir con vida.

Como solo, control remoto en mano,
y tengo todo un mundo en primer plano.
Noche tras noche, pasan la misma filmación

y la gran ola rompe sobre la vegetación
azotando las palmeras a la altura de los cocos.
Dan ganas de decir: paren un poco,
entre el agua y los árboles se perdió la proporción,
vuelvan a pasarlo, por favor.

Y aquí está de nuevo la gran ola.
Sobre la copa de los árboles rompe ahora
y ¡ay! se lleva todo lo que es mío:
esposa, hijos, casa, todo está perdido,
perdido, succionado a través de la línea de palmeras,
más allá del banco de arena, más allá de la rompiente,
fuera del alcance de lo que un humano puede o siente.

Lo primero que vieron
era que el mar había desaparecido, todo entero,
y tan rápido que dejó peces en cantidad
sobre la arena, un milagro imprevisto, algo antes
    nunca visto,
como si el deseo de un idiota se hiciera realidad,
y corrieron los niños a llenarse las manos de comida
entre risas y alborozo, absurdamente sorprendidos,
incapaces de atender los gritos
de los que les decían que volvieran. Entonces vino
    la ola.

Entonces vino la ola. Los pescadores que estaban mar
 adentro
sólo sintieron una fuerza verde que levantaba el bote
y que los dejó intactos y perfectamente a flote.
Sin embargo, para registrar la hora miraron el sol, allá
 arriba,
sin calibrar en ese instante todo lo que habían perdido:
esposa, hijos, casa, aldea, todo desaparecido
junto con cada rasgo familiar de su costa nativa...

Hasta que, invadidos por un miedo solemne por los suyos,
pusieron proa hacia la costa
y, al tocar tierra, mirándose entre sí,
arrastrando las quillas allí, donde antes era playa,
supieron en qué se habían convertido: una flota de
 viudos,
los suertudos, los ausentes,
solos, vivos entre árboles arrancados de raíz,
a los que los objetos de su amor no ofrecían bienvenida.

TSUNAMI
*translated by Yaki Setton and Sergio Waisman**

These furnishings are arrogant. They won't stop talking big.
I hide the crystal from the study and move chairs in the brig
and fill a bowl with colored fruit, so perfect
and I place it near the lamp,
I find a green vase and inside I shove
some anemones that create a nice effect.
None of this fools me even for a moment.
It barely helps me pass the time
but optimism I feel is not a crime
and the anemones know full well their task:
to open up in very deep blues and black.

Indulgent flowers:
slashed, packaged, they travel hours and hours without a rush
and reappear barely crushed.
And how quickly they recover their lushness!
Exemplary. In their intensity, so blue.
Too good to be true.
They almost make you happy with life's fullness.

I eat alone, control remote in hand,
and have a whole world on demand.

Night after night, they play the same recording
upon the vegetation the great wave pounding
whipping the palm trees at the height of the coconuts.
Makes you want to say: hold on, cut,
between the water and the trees proportion has been lost,
play it again, Sam.

And here again is the great wave.
Atop the tree-crowns it now breaks
and oh! it takes all that is mine:
all is lost, children, home, wife,
lost, suctioned through the line of palm trees,
beyond the sandbanks, beyond the breakers,
beyond the reach of what a human might, or feel.

The first thing they did see
was that the sea had disappeared, all of it entirely,
and so quickly it left fishes in a quantity
on the sand, an unforeseen miracle, something never
    before seen,
like the desire of an idiot become reality,
and the children ran for handfuls of rice and beans
between laughter and delight, surprised, absurdly
unable to pay attention to the screams
telling them to come back. Then the wave came.

Then the wave came. The fishermen who were offshore
only felt a green force lifting their boat
leaving them intact and perfectly afloat.
However, to note the time they looked at the sun, above,
without calibrating at that instant all they had lost:
all disappeared, children, home, wife, town,
along with every familiar trace of their native coast...

Until, invaded by a solemn fear for their own,
they aimed the prow toward the coast
and, upon touching land, looking at each other,
dragging the keels where the beach used to be,
they knew what they had become: a fleet of widowers,
the lucky ones, the absent ones,
alone, alive among trees pulled from their roots,
whom their objects of love did not welcome home.

---

* TRANSLATORS' NOTE: These are our direct translations of Mirta Rosenberg's Spanish-language versions of James Fenton's "Tsunami" and of Kay Ryan's "Things Shouldn't Be So Hard" and "Blandeur," extending the idea of "Conversos" that literary translations are creative writings in and of themselves. By including these translations of Rosenberg's translations, we invite the reader to access Rosenberg's versions of Fenton's and Ryan's poems as if they were originals.

THINGS SHOULDN'T BE SO HARD
Kay Ryan

A life should leave
deep tracks:
ruts where she
went out and back
to get the mail
or move the hose
around the yard;
where she used to
stand before the sink,
a worn-out place;
beneath her hand
the china knobs
rubbed down to
white pastilles;
the switch she
used to feel for
in the dark
almost erased.
Her things should
keep her marks.
The passage
of a life should show;
it should abrade.

And when life stops,
a certain space—
however small—
should be left scarred
by the grand and
damaging parade.
Things shouldn't
be so hard.

LAS COSAS NO DEBERÍAN SER TAN DURAS
translated by Mirta Rosenberg

Una vida debería dejar
profundas huellas:
surcos en el sitio
en que ella salía y volvía
para buscar el correo
o mover la manguera
en el jardín;
donde solía
pararse ante el fregadero,
un lugar desgastado;
bajo su mano,
los tiradores de porcelana
frotados hasta convertirse
en pastillas blancas;
el interruptor que solía
buscar tanteando
a oscuras
casi borrado.
Sus cosas tendrían
que conservar sus marcas.
El paso de una vida
debería verse;
mostrar su erosión.

Y cuando la vida se interrumpe,
un cierto espacio
—por pequeño que sea—
tendría que exhibir las cicatrices
de ese tránsito
grandioso y dañino.
Las cosas no tendrían
que ser tan duras.

Things Shouldn't be so Hard
translated by Yaki Setton and Sergio Waisman

A life should leave
deep prints:
grooves at the site
where she'd go out and back
to gather the mail
or move the hose
in the garden;
where she'd
stand before the sink,
a faded place;
under her hand,
the porcelain knobs
rubbed till they become
white pills;
the switch she'd
search for
in the dark
nearly erased.
Her things should
keep their marks.
The passing of a life
should be seen;
show its erosion.

And when life is switched off,
a certain space
—small as it may be—
should exhibit the scars
of that grand, damaging
transiting.
Things shouldn't have to
be so hard.

BLANDEUR
Kay Ryan

If it please God,
let less happen.
Even out Earth's
rondure, flatten
Eiger, blanden
the Grand Canyon.
Make valleys
slightly higher,
widen fissures
to arable land,
remand your
terrible glaciers
and silence
their calving,
halving or doubling
all geographical features
toward the mean.
Unlean against our hearts.
Withdraw your grandeur
from these parts.

INSIGNIFICANCIA
translated by Mirta Rosenberg

Si te place, Dios,
que menos ocurra.
Nivela la curvatura
de nuestra Tierra, aplana
el Eiger, suaviza
el Gran Cañón.
Haz los valles
un poco más altos,
amplía las fisuras
hasta que sean tierras cultivables,
custodia sus terribles glaciares
y silencia sus claudicaciones,
reduciendo a la mitad
o duplicando
todos los accidentes geográficos,
tendiendo a la humildad.
Deja de pasar sobre nuestros corazones.
Retira tu grandiosidad
de estas regiones.

INSIGNIFICANCE
translated by Yaki Setton and Sergio Waisman

If it please thee, God,
may it less occur.
Level the curvature
of our Earth, flatten
the Eiger, soften
the Grand Canyon.
Make the valleys
a little bit taller,
broaden the fissures
until they become arable lands,
watch over your terrible glaciers
and silence their claudications,
reducing by half
or doubling
all geographic accidents,
tending toward humility.
Quit weighing upon our hearts.
Withdraw your grandiosity
from these parts.

The Eye of the I:
Translating Mirta Rosenberg

Mirta Rosenberg (1951–2019) is a unique poet in Argentine—and in Latin American—letters. This is very much related to Rosenberg's work as a translator, and to the way she incorporates her readings of Anglo-American traditions in her own poetry. Rosenberg's poetry contains an unexpected word play that is at once colloquial and elevated. Her poems combine Argentine, idiomatic expressions with more literary, even anachronistic vocabulary, often taking tensions between form and content, between voice and body to the limit. Similarly, there is a simultaneity between the lyrical voice and a metatextual conscience which allows the poetic voice to question her place in and relationship to the world.

El paisaje interior [*Interior Landscape*] is the culmination of Rosenberg's work. Originally published in

Spanish in Buenos Aires, Argentina by Bajo la luna in 2012, it is the first book-length translation of Mirta Rosenberg's poetry to be published in English. The poems in the book explore the relationship between language and experience, how this relationship manifests in the body, and how all this changes with time. There is a tension between the autobiographical and the speaking voice. The poems in *Interior Landscape* work with an "I" that is personal and intimate; but the "I" also takes distance from what it says, and how it says it. As it does so, the poetic voice displays an interior landscape of a very well-read, rich experience, as well as the complex ways that language forms that experience.

But what, exactly, is an "interior landscape"? The English poet Gerard Manley Hopkins coined the term "inscape" in the late nineteenth century. Previously translated into Spanish as "essence," Mirta Rosenberg opts instead for "el paisaje interior" and uses it as the title for this book. In our version, in English, it becomes "interior landscape." Nearly but not quite an oxymoron, an "interior landscape" is a fascinating idea and, in the context of these poems, an intensified way of synthesizing Rosenberg's concept of subjectivity: a concise, sophisticated way to express everything that it means to say "I."

The central part of the book, entitled "Interior Landscape," contains an especially moving sequence of poems. Here, body and mind are at a crossroads due to a disease that left the poet unable to walk for the last years of her life. The poetic voice, the "I," reviews and reconstructs her "interior landscape" from her new "sedentary atmosphere," as she refers to it in one of the poems—remaining always implacable, defiant, never yielding to any dramatism. As the Spanish poet Olvido García Valdez says in her introduction to the Spanish edition of Rosenberg's poetry, the poems in Interior Landscape are: "assembled on the edge of sentiment and thought—where feeling and thinking are two sides of the same blade."

* * *

The English-language versions we present here are the result of a collaboration. As translators we were heartened, from the beginning, by the importance of translation in Rosenberg's poetry, and by the value of collaborative translation that Rosenberg found in her work. As Rosenberg has said: "I very much like translating with others. I like the dialogue created; the translation broaches essential points of the poetry for me; and, if there are two us, so much the better." In our case, we developed a process of collaboration that involved first drafts that tended to be fairly literal, followed by long sessions of working together (on Zoom), then rewriting and rereading and rewriting as many times as each poem seemed to require—sometimes, it felt, ad infinitum. Toward the end of the project, we were able to consult with Miguel Balaguer, Rosenberg's son and editor of Bajo la luna, in conversations that added another valuable layer to our reading of the poems.

The challenges to translating Rosenberg's poetry are numerous. Many were the times that we felt we were at a dead end; yet we would go back and reread and try and try again, until one of us would come up with something. For example, the first poem of the book, entitled "I" ("Yo"), ends with a verse that seems impossible to translate. The poem anticipates the main themes of the book, in terms of the relationship between emotions and language, establishing a tension between the grammatical "I" and the poetic voice of the "I." There is an unfolding of the first and the third person: "Turning error into virtue, / I'm where my head used to be, seeing all / as far as my eyes could see, / because she—not I—never got lost." This tension, this unfolding, extends to a consideration of the relationship between form and content; the poem concludes: "cobró la forma del contenido / agrandó la o del yo." Literally, this would be: "collected the form of the content / enlarged the o of the I." In the last verse, a literal translation would be especially senseless. The verses in the original highlight a key idea in the poem, related to the ability of the "I" to "see" in a union of mind and body, in a fusion of form and content. Finally, to translate the last verses, we focused on the resonances of the poem, not just its literal aspects. In the "o" of the "yo" we find a play between the visual and meaning. In Spanish this is primarily a typographical effect: expanded the "o" of the "yo." In our version in English, this becomes primarily a phonetic one: "took on the form of the content / expanded the eye of the I."

These tensions between the first and the third person, between form and content, are found throughout the book in rhymes and resonances, in Rosenberg's word play and changes of register. We sought to recreate the musicality, but it was not always in the same verses; our versions were not—they could not be—mirrors of the originals. But they could recreate the importance of rhymes and resonances—of the analogies in meanings created by the rhymes and resonances. The use of rhymes in the poems are, at times, playful and comical, reminiscent of Edward Lear's limericks and Lewis Carroll's nonsense verses. The challenge in these situations was to reproduce analogous effects, and to decide when nonsense did, in fact, communicate a certain kind of fragmented sense of its own kind. For example: "If Someone Would Like to be a Turtle / that would be me: / make from a section that's conical / my own headquarters, prehistorical, / lodged in the spinal cord." The seeming arbitrary playfulness of the "I" as a turtle coincides with an ambiguity about the body of both the poetic voice and the poet.

* * *

The central section of the book, entitled "Interior Landscape," as previously mentioned, also has an auto-referential element. All the poems in the section speak with the same poetic voice. This voice dialogues constantly with its body, a body that is forced to remain seated. A tension is generated between the inevitability of the situation—the subject must "sit down"—and the willingness of the "I" to go on nonetheless. This tension, in Spanish, is created with the repetition of the use of the infinitive, reflexive verb "sentarse" at the end of every poem in the sequence. "Sentarse y ..." thus functions as a kind of impersonal mandate to the self. Translating "sentarse" into English, in this context, had to include the mandate to oneself. There was also the limitation that English does not have reflexive verbs. How to translate, for example: "Sentarse y en una lista / ultimar la biografía"?

For "sentarse y ..." in English we opted for the second person imperative of a poetic voice speaking to herself: "Sit down and ...." The body of the "I" must sit down, but the voice tells it to "sit down" as if there were another choice—although, of course, there is no other choice. In this sense, we change the verb tenses (from infinitive, reflexive, third person to imperative, second person) but replicate as much as possible of the internal dialogue and the uncomfortable sense of the situation. Thus, in the example above, we arrived at: "Sit down and in a list / finish off the biography."

In the last section of the book, meanwhile, Rosenberg returns explicitly to the importance of translation in her poetry by including her versions of poems that, as she puts it, "have exercised an influence over [her] own writing." The title of this section, "Conversos," is significant in this regard: "conversos" is literally "converts," as in someone who has converted from one religion to another. Historically, "conversos" were Jews who were forced to convert to Catholicism in Spain or Portugal in the fourteenth and fifteenth centuries. But there is also a play on words: "con" "versos" sounds like "with" "verses", or "with-verses," or perhaps "con-versions." It is as if "Conversos" extended the conversation of her versions with the originals that have influenced her poetry. By doing so, Rosenberg highlights the idea that literary translations are creative writings in and of themselves. She is adding her twist, here, to a tradition exemplified by poets Robert Lowell and, in Argentina, Alberto Girri.

The "Conversos" section of the original publication of *El paisaje interior* included Rosenberg's translations into Spanish of A.K. Ramanujan's English-language translations of classical Tamil love poems; as well as Rosenberg's translations into Spanish of poems in English by Elizabeth Bishop, Robert Lowell, James Fenton, and Kay Ryan. In this edition, it was only possible to include Ramanujan's English-language translations besides Rosenberg's translations, along with three versions of James Fenton's and Kay Ryan's poems: the original poems in English, Rosenberg's translations into Spanish, and our translations into English of Rosenberg's Spanish-language versions.

* * *

It is typically said that something is always lost in translation, especially in the translation of poetry. But it is also true that something is always gained in translation. As collaborators, we were often aware of what we were unable to reproduce in our versions. We often had to make choices between trying to recreate aspects of the poem's form or of the poem's ideas and concepts. Sometimes we were aware of what our versions had gained, such as the example of the "eye of the I." We were always, however, very much aware that our translations were versions. What might be recovered in these versions? In the last sentence of the "Prologue" to "Conversos," the poet says: "Hopefully my versions bear at least a distant resemblance to the virtues of the poems." We would like to think the same about our versions of the gems in *Interior Landscape*: hopefully our versions bear at least a distant resemblance to the virtues of Mirta Rosenberg's poems.

Yaki Setton and Sergio Waisman
Buenos Aires and Silver Spring, Maryland—Madrid
April 2023

Mirta Rosenberg (Rosario, 1951–Buenos Aires, 2019) was an Argentine poet, translator, and editor. She developed a unique style, influenced in part by the British and US poets she translated, that manifests sharp emotional revelations and an intense subjectivity, while reflecting on the linguistic and formal construction of language itself. Her books of poetry include *Pasajes* (1984), *Madam* (1988), *Teoría sentimental* (1994), *El arte de perder* (1998), *El árbol de palabras* (2006), *El paisaje interior* (2012), the anthology *El arte de perder y otros poemas* (2015), and *Cuaderno de oficio* (2016). She was a key member of *Diario de Poesía* (1986–2012) and founded the prestigious independent press Bajo la luna in 1990. Her poetry has been included in numerous anthologies, and individual poems have been translated into English, French, and German. She was awarded, among others, a Guggenheim Poetry Fellowship and a Konex Foundation Award.

Yaki Setton was born in Buenos Aires, Argentina in 1961. He has published eight books of poetry, including *Quirurgia* (Paradiso), *Niñas* (Bajo la luna), *Nombres propios* (Bajo la luna), *La educación musical* (Bajo la luna), *Lej-Lejá* (Bajo la luna), *El beso* (Bajo la luna), and *Langosta* (Bajo la luna, 2023). An English-language version of *A Musical Education* (translated by Sergio

Waisman) was published as a chapbook by Toad Press in 2020. He is a Professor of Creative Writing at the University of Buenos Aires, Argentina.

Sergio Waisman has translated, among others, *The Underdogs* by Mariano Azuela (Penguin), three books by Ricardo Piglia, Juan José Saer's *The Regal Lemon Tree* (Open Letter Books), and three titles for Oxford's Library of Latin America. In 2000 he received an NEA Translation Fellowship Award for his work on Piglia's *The Absent City* (Duke). He is also the author of *Borges and Translation* (Bucknell), and the novels *Irse* (Bajo la luna) and *El encargo* (Mansalva). He is a Professor of Spanish and Latin American Literatures at The George Washington University.

"What She Said [Bigger than earth, certainly]," "What She Said [The still drone of time]," "What the Passers-by Said," "What the Concubine Said," "What the Foster-Mother Said," and "What He Said" from *The Interior Landscape* by A.K. Ramanujan. First published in English by New York Review Books. Translation Copyright © 2014 by A.K. Ramanujan.

"Tsunami" reprinted by kind permission of James Fenton.

"Things Shouldn't Be So Hard" from *The Niagara River* Copyright © 2005 by Kay Ryan. "Blandeur" from *Say Uncle* Copyright © 2000 by Kay Ryan. Used by permissions of Grove/Atlantic, Inc.

"Cat in Portrait," translated by Yaki Setton and Sergio Waisman, was first published in *The Paris Review*.

Printed & bound by Sheridan (Saline, MI)
Covers printed letterpress at Ugly Duckling Presse
Typesetting by Kireji

This project is supported in part by an award from
the National Endowment for the Arts, by a Poetry
Programs, Partnerships, and Innovation grant from the
Poetry Foundation, and by the New York State Council
on the Arts with the support of the Office of the
Governor and the New York State Legislature.

This work has been published within the framework
of the Sur Translation Support Programme of the
Ministry of Foreign Affairs, International Trade and
Worship of the Argentine Republic. / Obra editada en
el marco del Programa Sur de Apoyo a las Traducciones
del Ministerio de Relaciones Exteriores, Comercio
Internacional y Culto de la República Argentina.